For Alex, in so many ways

Published by Charlesbridge
9 Galen Street
Watertown, MA 02472
(617) 926-0329
www.charlesbridge.com

Library of Congress Cataloging-in-Publication Data
Names: O'Brien, Patrick, 1960– author, illustrator.
Title: Big babies / Patrick O'Brien.
Description: Watertown, MA: Charlesbridge, [2024] |
    Audience: Ages 3-7 | Audience: Grades K-1 | Summary:
    "Before dinosaurs were big, most of them came from
    small eggs and were tiny but mighty babies."–Provided
    by publisher.
Identifiers: LCCN 2022031343 (print) | LCCN 2022031344
    (ebook) | ISBN 9781623543662 (hardcover) |
    ISBN 9781632893451 (ebook)
Subjects: LCSH: Dinosaurs–Infancy–Juvenile literature. |
    Dinosaurs–Juvenile literature.
Classification: LCC QE861.5 .O27 2024 (print) | LCC QE861.5
    (ebook) | DDC 567.9–dc23/eng20230203
LC record available at https://lccn.loc.gov/2022031343
LC ebook record available at https://lccn.loc.gov/2022031344

Printed in China
(hc) 10 9 8 7 6 5 4 3 2 1

Illustrations produced with digital media
Display type set in Grilled Cheese © Bitstream Inc. and
    Font Diner, designed by Stuart Sandler
Text type set in Mikado © Hannes von Döhren
Printed by 1010 Printing International Limited in Huizhou,
    Guangdong, China
Production supervision by Jennifer Most Delaney
Designed by Cathleen Schaad

PATRICK O'BRIEN

BIG BABIES

🌉 Charlesbridge

SEISMOSAURUS
"earthquake lizard"

This small giant grew into a lumbering leaf-eater that shook the ground with its tremendous weight.

TYRANNOSAURUS REX
"tyrant lizard king"

This tiny toddler grew up to be a mighty meat-eating monster. In the years that the tyrannosaurus roamed Earth, it was a top predator.

ANATOTITAN

"giant duck"

This dinosaur's snout looked a bit like a duck's beak. Inside this flattened snout were hundreds of teeth, perfect for munching prehistoric plants.

TRICERATOPS
"three-horned face"

This lively little imp grew up to be a jumbo-sized, bad-tempered titan. It had one of the biggest skulls in the dinosaur world.

MICROPACHYCEPHALO-SAURUS

"small, thick-headed lizard"

This was one of the smallest dinosaurs, but it had the longest name. The bony dome on top of its head was for battling other micropachycephalosaurs.

SUPERSAURUS
"super lizard"

This scaly dinosaur grew to be one of the biggest of all the dinosaurs. The super-sized supersaurus was a giant among giants.

VELOCIRAPTOR
"swift thief"

This feathery dino grew into a fearsome, high-speed hunter, with a big sharp claw on each back foot.

ELASMOSAURUS
"thin-plate reptile"

Elasmosaurus swam through ancient waters on four flapping flippers. It used its long, snaky neck and big, spiky teeth to feast on fish.

STEGOSAURUS
"roofed lizard"

This pint-sized critter grew into a leaf-eater
that had a body the size of an elephant but
a brain the size of a meatball.

PTERANODON
"winged and toothless"

This lanky little flyer soared above the dinosaurs on leathery wings. Its long beak was perfect for dipping into the water to catch yummy fish.

MEI LONG
"sleeping dragon"

This mini dragon lived near big, fire-breathing volcanoes. It was one of the smallest dinosaurs.

The name *dinosaur* means "terrible lizard" in the Greek language. But this name is misleading. Even though *saurus* means "lizard," dinosaurs were not lizards. When the first few dinosaur bones were discovered, scientists thought that the bones must have belonged to some kind of ancient lizard. But now, after many more discoveries, scientists have learned that dinosaurs were not lizards. Dinosaurs were reptiles, and lizards are a different kind of reptile.

Seismosaurus

Seismosaurus was a kind of dinosaur called a sauropod. There were many kinds of sauropods, and they were all plant-eaters, with a small head compared to their long neck and tail. The adult seismosaurus could weigh as much as fifteen elephants and could be as long as a football field. It needed a massive amount of greenery to feed its massive body.

Tyrannosaurus rex

Scientists believe a T-rex hatchling was about the size of a goose, but its parents were giants that terrorized the dinosaur world. Tyrannosaurus arms were very small, but their huge jaws and big fangs did most of the work.

Anatotitan

Anatotitan was a kind of dinosaur called a hadrosaur. Large herds of these duck-billed beasts roamed the dinosaur world, munching tons of plants with their hundreds of teeth.

Triceratops

An adult triceratops was about thirty feet long. The three huge horns on its face allowed it to do battle with the fiercest predators. It also had a strong shield made of solid bone on the back of its head for extra protection.

Micropachycephalosaurus

This small dinosaur was named for its thick skull. *Micro* means small, *pachy* means thick, and *cephalo* means head. Scientists think that the creature used its thick, bony skull to ram into the skulls of others of its kind.

Supersaurus

Supersaurus was a kind of sauropod dinosaur. It grew over 100 feet long—as long as a blue whale, which is the largest animal on Earth today! While all sauropods were huge, and the biggest of these giants are called supergiants, no one quite knows how or why these animals became so big.

Velociraptor

The feathery velociraptor was a very bird-like reptile, even though it couldn't fly. It grew to be about the size of a turkey, and its skeleton and body looked a lot like those of modern birds. In fact, birds evolved from dinosaurs like the velociraptor. This means that some dinosaurs—like the velociraptor—changed over time to become the birds we know today.

Elasmosaurus

Elasmosaurus was not a dinosaur—it was a different kind of reptile that coexisted with many dinosaurs. It lived in the sea, but it had to come up for air like dolphins and seals do today. Its elongated neck was longer than the rest of its body.

Stegosaurus

An adult stegosaurus was about the size of an elephant. It had large, flat bony plates along its back. Four sharp spikes lined the end of its tail and helped fight off any predators looking for a big meal.

Pteranodon

Pteranodon was not a dinosaur. It was a kind of pterosaur—a large group of flying reptiles that lived at the same time as many dinosaurs. It flew on long, leathery wings that were stretched between its body, arms, and long pinky bones. Scientists believe a pteranodon hatchling had a one-foot wingspan.

Mei long

The fossils of this little dinosaur were found in China. Because these bones showed that the creature had been curled up in a sleeping position with its head tucked under an arm and its tail wrapped around its body, scientists named it "sleeping dragon" in Mandarin. This was one of the smallest dinosaurs. Even full grown, the Mei long was only about the size of a duck. Scientists know that the juvenile Mei long was about twenty-one inches long. But a hatchling would have been significantly smaller.

BEHOLD THE BABIES!

Compared to the size of a four-foot tall kid.

Seismosaurus

Tyrannosaurus rex

Anatotitan

Triceratops

Micropachycephalosaurus

Human